The 5 Minute

To-Do List Formula

A Diagrammatic Guide To Complete Your Tasks Within 2 Weeks

The 5 Minute Self Help Series (Book 2)

Magnus Muller

Text Copyright © Magnus Muller

All rights reserved. No part of this guide may be reproduced in any form without permission in writing from the publisher except in the case of brief quotations embodied in critical articles or reviews.

Legal & Disclaimer

The information contained in this book and its contents is not designed to replace or take the place of any form of medical or professional advice; and is not meant to replace the need for independent medical, financial, legal or other professional advice or services, as may be required. The content and information in this book has been provided for educational and entertainment purposes only.

The content and information contained in this book has been compiled from sources deemed reliable, and it is accurate to the best of the Author's knowledge, information and belief. However, the Author cannot guarantee its accuracy and validity and cannot be held liable for any errors and/or omissions. Further, changes are periodically made to this book as and when needed. Where appropriate and/or necessary, you must consult a professional (including but not limited to your doctor, attorney, financial advisor or such other professional advisor) before using any of the suggested remedies, techniques, or information in this book.

Upon using the contents and information contained in this book, you agree to hold harmless the Author from and against any damages, costs, and expenses, including any legal fees potentially resulting from the application of any of the information provided by this book. This disclaimer applies to any loss, damages or injury caused by the use and application, whether directly or indirectly, of any advice or information presented, whether for breach of contract, tort, negligence, personal injury, criminal intent, or under any other cause of action.
You agree to accept all risks of using the information presented inside this book.

You agree that by continuing to read this book, where appropriate and/or necessary, you shall consult a professional (including but not limited to your doctor, attorney, or financial advisor or such other advisor as needed) before using any of the suggested remedies, techniques, or information in this book.

The 5 Minute Self Help Series

The 5 Minute Self Help Series (Book 1)

The 5 Minute Procrastination Addiction Cure
Eliminating Procrastination By Starting In 5 Minutes Or Less

By Magnus Muller

Kindle: http://www.amazon.com/dp/B07CT215ZZ
Paperback: http://www.amazon.com/dp/1983161640

The 5 Minute Self Help Series (Book 2)

The 5 Minute To-Do List Formula
A Diagrammatic Guide To Complete Your Task Within 2 Weeks

By Magnus Muller

Kindle: http://www.amazon.com/dp/B07F8HFDLC
Paperback: http://www.amazon.com/dp/1983360260

The 5 Minute Self Help Series (Book 3)

The 5 Minute Mindfulness Practical Guide
20 Simple Habits To Lead A Stress Free Life, Reduce Anxiety And Treat Depression

By Magnus Muller

Kindle: http://www.amazon.com/dp/B07F8H6ZS2
Paperback: http://www.amazon.com/dp/1983360392

Author's message

After embarking on my first book, "The 5 Minute Procrastination Addiction Cure", I have decided to embark on my second book, "The 5 Minute To Do List Formula".

Many people rely heavily on their To-Do Lists to complete their daily tasks. This book is for everyone, including youngsters, housewives and the working adults, to complete their daily tasks with ease through designing a simple To-Do List everyday.

The main focus of this book is not on procrastination and will not be a rehash of the content provided in my first book. But rather, this book will allow you to understand why you are failing in your To-Do List and will show you the step by step guide to designing a perfect To-Do List everyday so as to complete your tasks.

For each step in the solution, diagrams have been added where appropriate to guide you through the designing of this simple To-Do List. I hope that with these diagrams, you will able to follow the steps much more smoothly and design your To-Do List with ease.

Enjoy your read and I hope that after reading this book, you will be able to get on with your To-Do List and gain more time freedom while completing all your tasks.

Table of Contents

The 5 Minute Self Help Series 5

Author's message 9

Introduction 13

Chapter 1: Why do you fail to complete tasks even with a To-Do List? 17

The total confusion about the concept of a To-Do List 18

A look into a typical "To-Do List" 19

What you have to do to ensure that your To-Do List works 20

Chapter 2: Three examples of the most popular To-Do Lists 23

1: The 80/20 rule 24

2: The theory of the two factors 26

3: "I need, I should, I want" 28

Reasons why these methods may not be effective for some people 29

Chapter 3: A step-by-step guide to design a To-Do List in five minutes 31

Things to note before creating the To-Do List 32

Five simple steps to create your To-Do List under five minutes 34

Chapter 4: How to make your To-Do List sustainable 49

Types of distractions 50

The three main rules before applying the techniques 53

Techniques to stay focused when creating your To-Do List 54

Chapter 5: Tips to help save time in your daily tasks 59

Three main tips to save time when doing daily tasks 60

The difference between the urgent and the important 62

Conclusion 67

About the author 71

Leave a review 72

The 5 Minute Self Help Series 73

Check out other books 76

Introduction

How many times have you excitedly planned goals and objectives, only to end up quitting after a while, feeling guilty, and thinking that you have no willpower and that you are unable to follow plans through?

Although this is something very common that happens to all of us, the reality is that you don't have a problem. You're perfectly capable of finishing what you start and achieving your goals. The problem is not you but rather the methods you use; specifically, these are some of the reasons that make it difficult for you to achieve some of your goals and objectives.

To be productive and successful, it's not just about checking boxes on your To Do List, or trying to make a long list without knowing where to start. Instead, it's about making sure you're doing the right things, at the right time, on the right calendar, successfully and effectively. It's very important to have a good system, organized life and an effective workflow—not only for your work but also your personal life.

That is why I have prepared a practical guide to making a To-Do List. Start setting realistic goals, breaking those goals into actionable tasks, then at the end you can tell yourself: "I achieved something meaningful with a measurable impact."

This book is the perfect tool for you. In the next few chapters, I will guide you through the steps that will help you increase your productivity and build an efficient workflow. This includes:

- ✓ How to establish a To-Do List of productivity using the best techniques;
- ✓ Examples of most popular To-Do List, but reasons why those are not effective for everyone;
- ✓ How to prioritize tasks efficiently in a reasonable time;
- ✓ A step-by-step guide to designing a To-Do List in five minutes.

So, if you want to increase your productivity and be successful, what do you expect but to continue reading this book? Keep reading.

Enjoy!!!

Chapter 1: Why do you fail to complete tasks even with a To-Do List?

Many people, including you, have failed to use a To-Do List effectively. Most do it with the expectation of getting a sense of order and, of course, to carry out incomplete tasks. Not everyone experiences that feeling of being organized, but everyone longs for it. Having a clear and organized idea of your responsibilities, of what you have to do, will allow you to resolve matters calmly and get things done in a precise way.

You realize that sometimes, despite the fact that everything is apparently under control, the To-Do List resists—you cannot cross out tasks and the commitments continue accumulating one after the other. Finally, when you see that the To-Do List does not seem to work, you stop writing things down and try to keep going as usual ... until the next crisis.

The total confusion about the concept of a To-Do List

All of us who have spent time studying personal productivity have heard and read many times that "the best tool to improve productivity is to use a To-Do List". Common sense, right? Well, let me tell you that—as is often the case—to think that a productive practice is simply common sense (i.e. anyone can do it without thinking too much) is the first step towards failing miserably. While it is true that a To-Do List is something very simple to make, it is much harder to do it well and see it through.

A look into a typical "To-Do List"

Most of what people call "To-Do Lists" are actually amorphous and fragmented masses of desires—things they need, pending activities, reminders and commitments.

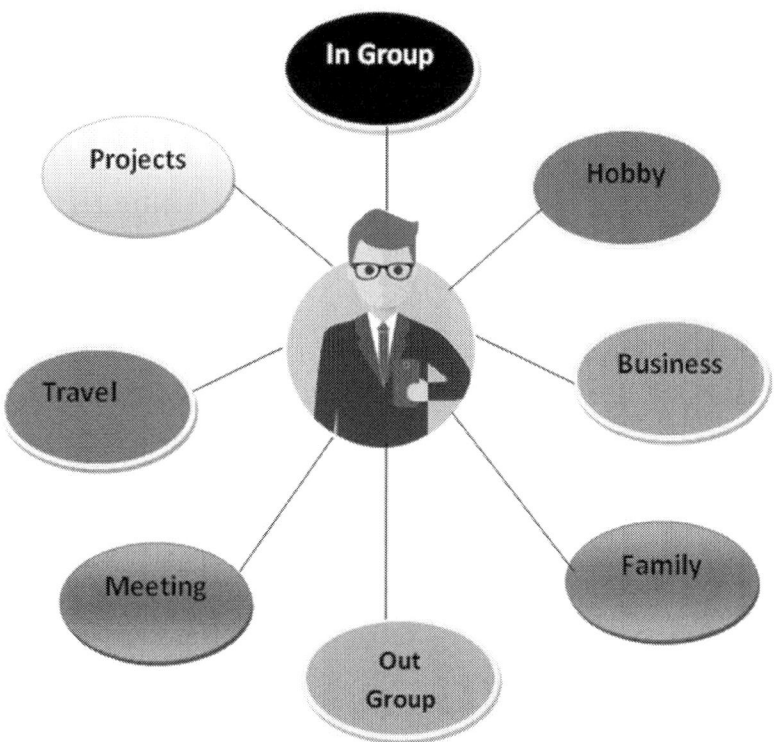

Let's take for example the task "prepare a report". Apparently, we are clear about what we need to do, right? We have a verb: *the action*; and a noun: *the result we want to obtain*. Everything seems ready to start... but it doesn't really work. What's going on?

What you have to do to ensure that your To-Do List works

If your subconscious realizes that information is missing, or that it is not sure about what needs to be done, it will resist—it's as simple as that. And it's very easy to check: there are always tasks on your To-Do List that you systematically skip over and over again, no matter how urgent they may be.

In order to unblock your mind and fix the situation, you first have to clarify what the task means and the first physical action that you have to carry out. In the previous example, although "*prepare*" is a verb, it doesn't constitute a specific concrete action that you can do, and your subconscious knows it. What does "prepare" really mean? Is it about getting yourself ready to write the report? Do you already have the structure clear? Do you already have the necessary information? And if you don't, do you know how to get it or who can you ask?

By asking the right questions, what previously seemed like a clear task now begins to take the form of what we so call a project, or set of physical actions aimed at obtaining a result. In other words, "prepare a report" is not a specific action that you can start.

The central problem is that our ranking of importance is too broad, so the To-Do List of high-priority items becomes too big: everything seems important. Or perhaps the To-Do List seems to focus on the wrong things at the wrong time. We often give up soon after, with the feeling that it's just not working. And so we fall back into overwhelming feelings of frustration and even guilt for not being able to keep up.

Chapter 2: Three examples of the most popular To-Do Lists

The methodologies of task organization are intended to help you organize yourself effectively and in a simple way to do all the tasks you have to complete—whether in your personal, academic or professional life—allowing you to plan, order and prioritize your work and avoid the trap of procrastination. But what happens if you don't choose the best method? You would agree with me if I told you that you would fail. That's why in this chapter, I'm going to show you some of the most popular To-Do Lists that aren't actually effective for most people.

1: The 80/20 rule

The 80/20 rule, also known as the Pareto Principle, tells us that only about 20% of activities produce 80% of the results. At that level of productivity, the rule implies that we need to debug numerous irrelevant tasks and inconsequential actions that don't generate the desired results.

How does it work?

The basic summary of the Pareto Principle is to identify in all areas of your daily life what is really important and focus your efforts on doing it as best you can. The least relevant tasks should be discarded, delegated or grouped to be carried out within a certain timeframe.

Take a pen and paper, and list that 20% of activities that produce 80% of your results. You can make the estimate based on professional benefits, economic compensation or profitability.

Manage your time properly so that the bulk of your work is allocated to that 20%: You must influence those tasks that give you better results, eliminate inefficient tasks as much as possible, and reduce the time spent on distractions such as emails or social media.

You have several options with respect to the 80%: Eliminate the tasks that you can, delegate what you can or group them in blocks to reduce the time you dedicate to them.

With this principle you, will learn to:

- ✓ Make decisions. You have to determine which of your tasks are really important.
- ✓ Concentrate your efforts on those important tasks to obtain greater profitability.
- ✓ Focus better.
- ✓ Work effectively by doing fewer tasks in less time.

2: The theory of the two factors

The theory of two factors was formulated by Frederick Herzberg to better explain the behavior of people in work situations. The author raises the existence of two factors that guide the behavior of people.

Firstly, satisfaction is mainly the result of motivation factors, which contribute to increase the satisfaction of the individual, but have little effect on dissatisfaction.

Secondly, dissatisfaction is mainly the result of hygiene factors. If these factors are missing or inadequate, they cause dissatisfaction, but their presence has a very little effect on long-term satisfaction.

Thus, applied to the field of work and productivity, this theory suggests that a worker should be in a place where there are (at the least) adequate working conditions, attractive salaries, and labor relations based on trust and flexibility—but also work that allows challenges and generates in the worker a sense of recognition and achievement. While money is not everything, the theory recommends that companies provide:

- ✓ Innovative and accessible workspaces: It is important to have ample space with zones for gamification, lunch and leisure to allow workers to develop freely, independently and collaboratively.

- ✓ A good organizational environment: Companies should nurture a positive corporate culture, encouraging feedback and trust among the team of employees.

- ✓ Possibilities for growth and personal development: It is essential that there are opportunities for promotion, recognition of professional tasks, responsibilities and new challenges.

- ✓ Hollow for creativity: Creative sessions such as hackathons, brainstorming and alternative ways ideas to propose ideas should be common within your company.

Not everyone agrees with this theory. Some critics have noted a series of negative or counterproductive effects, such as increased anxiety, increased conflict between expectations and reality, feelings of exploitation when the company delegate new tasks without increasing remuneration, possible reduction of interpersonal relationships, etc.

3: "I need, I should, I want"

"I need, I should, I want" is the method proposed by Jay Shirley. Jay developed a web application called "The Daily Practice", whose main purpose is to create habits based on three obligatory tasks. This technique consists in making a list each morning with three tasks: a task with high priority that will immediately impact your life ("I need"), a task destined to your long-term goals ("I should") and something that you feel like doing a lot throughout the day to contribute to your motivation ("I want").

To be effective, you must review the list the next morning. Have you managed to progress and be happy thanks to that list? However, it is essential not to need a daily incentive to sustain your high productivity rates.

Reasons why these methods may not be effective for some people

Many people endorse certain methods, but these methods don't always work for others. Why aren't these methods effective for everyone?

Well, let's review the first method mentioned above. The most important thing about the Pareto Principle and the best way to take advantage of it is to focus efforts and concentration on 20% of the relevant activities and situations. Unfortunately, the problem is that it's not often easy to know if we are focusing on said 20%.

Secondly is Herzberg's theory of two factors: satisfaction and dissatisfaction. However, those who practice this method are not always successful. Many fail in that model. Why? Because this method generates internal conflict and reduction of interpersonal relationships.

What is the common problem with these methods? It's that these assignation methods generally rank tasks not according importance, but urgency. By assigning priorities to the most urgent, the less urgent things end up being neglected and never realized; never, until a crisis occurs and, then, they become urgent.

So, if the most popular To-Do List methods aren't effective for some people—perhaps including you—how can you make your To-Do Lists effective? It is easy to do it thanks to a practical step-by-step guide that I will give you in the next chapter. Keep reading!

Chapter 3: A step-by-step guide to design a To-Do List in five minutes

There is no better feeling than crossing something off your To-Do List. Done! Finished! Mission complete! And yet it's easy to let a whole day or even a week go by without deleting any tasks from your To-Do List. How does that happen? Well, your To-Do List can be a tool that guides you through your work, or it can be a big pile of time bombs that are stalking you and your productivity. Everything depends on how you write it.

Think about your To-Do List as a series of instructions given by your Boss to your Assistant. Like a good computer program, if the instructions are clear, specific and easy to do, you will not have any problems. Otherwise, you will have many results that you didn't want, such as fear, procrastination and disappointment. Keep reading to discover how to create your very easy To-Do List in just five minutes.

Things to note before creating the To-Do List

When it's time to add something to your To-Do List, think about what you're going to write with the following points in mind.

Point 1: You're your own Boss and Assistant

At any time during your workday, you're in one of two modes: Thinking mode (when you have the Boss's cap on) and action mode (when you have the Assistant's cap). When a project or task arrives, the steps needed develop little by little in your mind. At that moment, you are in thinking mode as the person who gives the orders. Your To-Do List is a collection of those commands, which your Assistant personality will take and perform.

When you have the Boss's cap on, it is up to you to write the instructions in such a way that your Assistant personality can follow them without having to think or stress. Removing the thought behind the action is one of the best ways to make your To-Do List something very easy to perform.

Point 2: Just list the tasks you're definitely going to do

Sometimes you might think of tasks that you just aren't ready to do yet. Maybe learning a new language, even if it's an eventual goal, doesn't fit into your current situation. Maybe updating your website is a low priority because your business is changing other bigger things, so any changes to the site will be temporary or may not be needed for six months.

Instead of including tasks you aren't going to spend time on your To-Do List until you're tired of seeing them (and remembering that you haven't done them yet), move them to a separate list, an area for things that can wait. Only tell your Assistant-self to do something if you are absolutely sure that you can dedicate time to it, so there should only be concrete actions which you're sure to finish.

After seeing the instructions, let's jump right there to the 5 simple steps to create your To-Do List.

Five simple steps to create your To-Do List under five minutes

As these five steps may be unfamiliar to most of you, it may take up to even 30 minutes for you to absorb all the information and tips given here. However, you do not need to worry because as long as you follow these five steps daily, you will very soon find these steps simple and easy to follow. You will be surprised that after a while, you will be able to create your own To-Do List every day in just five minutes and complete your daily tasks after two weeks of using this To-Do List.

Step #1: Break down tasks

The fastest route to a creating task that you will avoid working on: making a vague monstrosity. If you write ambiguous things like "clean the office" on your to-do list, I guarantee it will be the last thing you start working on. In fact, "cleaning the office" is not even a task, it is a project.

As David Allen, author of "Getting Things Done" says: "Projects are not tasks; they are a collection of tasks."

That is an important difference. You should know that your To-Do List is not your list of projects. Don't write tasks like "clean the office" that require multiple actions. Break down projects into smaller and easier instructions such as "clear out the trash bin", "throw old papers" and "put old books in boxes".

If your Assistant personality asks "What do you want to be done?" and your Boss personality simply says "Clean the office", that will not get you anywhere.

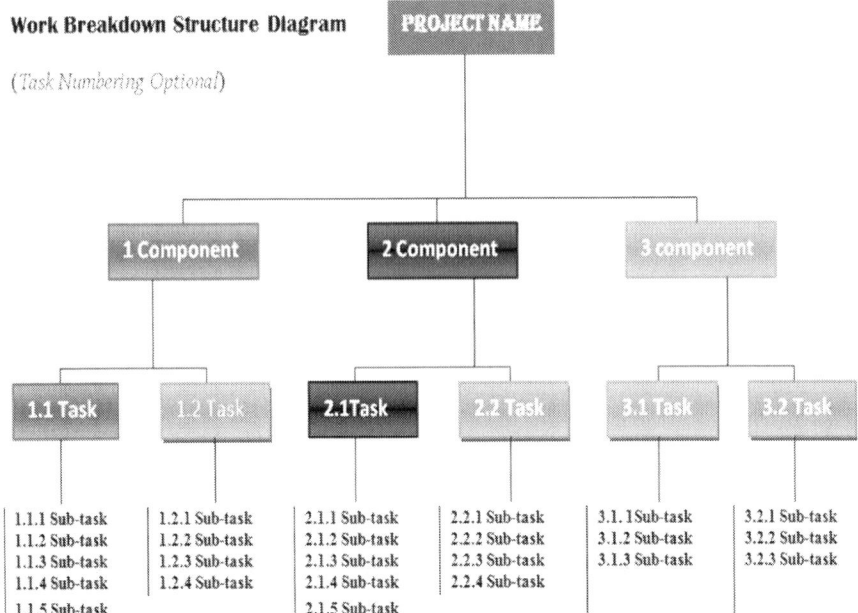

There are three points to note while creating your sub-tasks. They are:

- Make your sub-tasks easy instead of vague.
- Use specific and active verbs in your sub-tasks.
- Include as much as information as possible in the sub-tasks.

Point 1: Make your sub-tasks easy instead of vague

The smaller these sub-tasks are, the easier it will be for you to do them. The inspirational writer SARK breaks down her tasks into increments of five minutes and calls them "micromotions".

She says: "Micromotions are small steps you can take to complete things in your life. I am a procrastinator in recovery and I have few attention spans, so I invented micromovements as a method to complete projects in five minutes or less. I always feel that I can work with anything for five minutes."

Getting to those small tasks requires that you think before you write them on your To-Do List. The following examples contrast vague tasks (the type that create blockages) alongside their easy-to-do counterparts:

Vague Tasks	Easy tasks
Find a new dentist	Ask Sara what dentist she is going to
Replace the glass of the table	Take measurements of the table. Call Quick Glasses at 998-2123245 with the dimensions
Learn Italian	Check the X website (x.com) to see if they offer Italian classes
Update your website	Write a list of five improvements for your website

As you can see, breaking down your tasks into smaller actions creates more than one task for things that are in fact small projects. For example, replacing the glass of a table involves measuring the table, calling and asking for a replacement, then possibly going to pick it up—which brings you to your next step.

Point 2: Use specific and active verbs in your sub-tasks

When you tell yourself to do something, make it an order. Something like "Company's Account Review" doesn't tell you what to do. Write your tasks with specific actions, such as "Call Robert at the company to enquire about the 2nd-month sales". Make sure you don't use the word "contact". Use "call". Contact can mean telephone, email, etc.; but your verbs should be as specific as possible. Imagine yourself literally instructing an Assistant on their first day of work about what you need them to do.

Point 3: Include as much information as possible in the sub-tasks

When you formulate your To-Do List, your job as a Boss is to make it as easy as possible for your Assistant to do the work. For example, if you have to make a call, include the name or number. Instead of "Donate the old furniture," write "Call David to schedule the furniture, 55-5234-1246." When you're stuck in a waiting room with only your phone, you cannot donate your old furniture, but of course you can make a call, if you have the phone. Be a good Boss. Make sure your Assistant has all the necessary resources to do the job.

Step #2: Prioritize your tasks

It is common to see that our To-Do List often have as much as 20 tasks, but the reality is that you will only manage to do a few per day (assuming you aren't writing things like "get up, have a shower, make coffee, go to work"—which you really shouldn't be listing). So make sure that the most important tasks are on top of your list. How you do this depends on which tool or software you use for your list, but make sure you can quickly see what you should do next (better start with a pen and paper!).

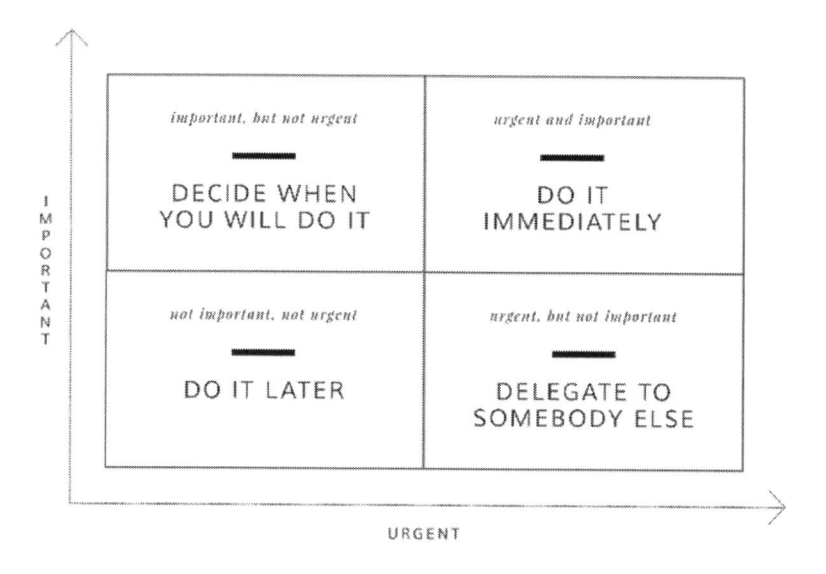

	important, but not urgent	*urgent and important*
IMPORTANT	DECIDE WHEN YOU WILL DO IT	DO IT IMMEDIATELY
	not important, not urgent	*urgent, but not important*
	DO IT LATER	DELEGATE TO SOMEBODY ELSE

URGENT

After you have written the sub-tasks (as shown in Step #1), now draw the same diagram as the one above, insert those sub-tasks into the four respective boxes.

Step #3: Create, clean and update your To-Do List

After you have listed the various sub-tasks and divided them, create a To-Do List like the one below:

To-Do List

PRIORITY	DEADLINE	WHAT	IN PROGRESS	DONE
Urgent	16/06/2018	Electricity to be paid	X	
Important	16/06/2018	Clean up the office		X
Not important	16/06/2018	Shopping	X	
Urgent	16/06/2018	Fix the car		X
Important	16/06/2018	Bring child to school	X	
Urgent	16/06/2018	Go to see my Mom	X	
Urgent	16/06/2018	Go to the hospital		X
Not important	16/06/2018	Go to the Gym	X	
Important	16/06/2018	Prepare the breakfast		X

You can arrange your sub-tasks by deadline, then by priority. Mark out those that are "In Progress" and "Done". However, in addition to prioritizing, you must accommodate your tasks by age. What elements have been on your list the longest? You probably have a mental block with tasks that have been there a long time, so you must go back to work on them or break them down even more. Or maybe you shouldn't do them after all. (Remember, removing an item from your To-Do List is even better than marking it as complete because you've saved yourself the time and effort.)

After you have completed your To-Do List, you will need to routinely clean and update your To-Do List as necessary.

Just as a manager would meet with their team once a week, schedule a 20-minute meeting with yourself every Monday or Friday to review your To-Do List, projects, and list of things you want to do someday.

This short weekly ritual can help you feel comfortable with your tasks.

I've included an example of a updated To-Do List below. Clean up those tasks that are already done, as well as those that are not important, and replace them for others.

To-Do List

PRIORITY	DEADLINE	WHAT	IN PROGRESS	DONE
Urgent	16/06/2018	Electricity to be paid	X	
Important	16/06/2018	Bring child to school	X	
Urgent	16/06/2018	Go to see my Mom	X	
Urgent	16/06/2018	Meditate	X	
Important	16/06/2018	Others	X	

You may wish to skip this step of reviewing your To-Do List if all the tasks are all due that same day. Then all you have to do is to mark those completed tasks as "Done" and create a new To-Do List the next day.

If your To-Do List includes tasks that have long deadlines (e.g. a week later), then either break those tasks into sub-tasks with separate daily deadlines (e.g. break it down to five sub-tasks and complete one sub-task each day for a total of five days), or simply keep those tasks in your To-Do List till the overall task is done.

Step #4: Record your completed tasks

Like any good Assistant, you want to show your Boss exactly everything you've done. Make sure you write your complete elements somewhere so that you can measure your own productivity and use it as a reference point. Your list of completed tasks is a good indicator of whether your To-Do List method is working. If you spend more than two days without any new items, it's time to review your list and improve it.

PRIORITY	DEADLINE	WHAT	IN PROGRESS	DONE
Important	16/06/2018	Clean up the office		X
Urgent	16/06/2018	Fix the car		X
Important	16/06/2018	Go to the hospital		X
Urgent	16/06/2018	Prepare the breakfast		X

Step #5: Practice makes perfect

This means that you must move from theory to practice, and apply the knowledge of this book to the real world. This may seem like a long list of rules for something as simple as a To-Do List, but 90% of the work needed to complete important tasks is the planning part—and that's true even for tasks that seem more trivial.

In this chapter, we have seen five practical steps to create an effective To-Do List. Do your best to move quickly and efficiently according to this. Don't postpone. The list will always be waiting—and the longer you wait, the more difficult it can be to complete some of those tasks. Taking a break is fine, but remember that the sooner you do the work, the sooner you can concentrate on what you really want to do!

What do you have to do to stay on the right track while creating a To-Do List? How do you stay focused or concentrate to create your To-Do List? In the next chapter, I will teach you how to do so. Keep reading.

Chapter 4: How to make your To-Do List sustainable

I understand you perfectly—it is extremely frustrating not to finish or move forward with your To-Do List. Many times, although your surroundings are optimal for work or study, it is your thoughts that sabotage your best attempts to concentrate. Trying to dodge the many distractions, excuses, etc., seems an impossible mission that only ninjas with great mastery of mind can achieve.

However, the good thing is that this chapter is the right path for you. In this chapter, I'll explain how to train your mind to concentrate better in order to stick to the right path while creating the correct To-Do List.

Before that, it is essential for you to recognize that in order to keep this To-Do List sustainable, you must stay focus and not be distracted. Let me bring you through the 2 main types of distraction and how to stay focused instead.

Types of distractions

There are two classifications for all those distractions:

1. External distractions: unexpected visits, phone calls, spontaneous commitments, emails, mobile notifications, messages, etc.

2. Internal distractions: thoughts, desires, impulses, worries, and ideas.

You may notice that the internal are relatively few, but these are the most problematic for a simple reason: because you create them yourself. They are the product of your cognition, your thoughts and your memories.

All start with a thought that appears in your mind. For example: "How many?" "I like this." "What about my pictures on Facebook, Twitter, and Instagram?" The impulse is so great that you can't resist following the course of this thought, which distracts you. It is only when you manage to control your own mind that you can easily avoid these kinds of thoughts.

But the question that many people ask is: Why can't we control these thoughts? Why do we lose control of the rudder and lose our attention? The answer is simple. It's because in your daily life, you train your brain to be distracted without realizing.

ADD (Attention Deficit Disorder) is a psychological condition whereby people are unable to concentrate on something for extended periods of time. Although this condition is fairly common, not everyone suffers it.

Ed Hallowell, a former professor at Harvard Medical School, says that we have generated a "cultural attention deficit."

We have trained our brains to change attention over and over again, losing the ability to focus on one thing.

Bouncing between one activity and another seems like merely a bad habit; however, it is even more than that. These abrupt changes of attention between activities weaken your mental strength to keep your attention on one thing. You become addicted to variety and compulsively wish to direct your attention to something new, such as a spontaneous thought, a notification, or a new activity.

The problem is that when we really want to concentrate, it is impossible. Your mind laughs out loud, thinking it's a joke. Satisfying the deep desire to distract yourself is like spoiling your mind to instant gratification.

While it sounds strange, it is normal to fight against your deepest desires all the time. According to a study, the three main desires against which we fight all day are: sex, sleep and eating. But the list also includes the desire to distract you with a rewarding, easy and novel activity.

How do you train your mind to concentrate on just two steps when creating your To-Do List?

It seems like an easy question to answer. But be careful, as there are thousands of tips trying to address that question that don't really work. Everything depends on the type of activity. So, then, I'm going to explain three main rules before seeing what techniques you can use to increase your concentration.

The three main rules before applying the techniques

Rule #1: Your activity doesn't have to be a usual distraction

Many activities are discarded because they don't train your attention but weaken it. For example, if you constantly have the impulse to check your mail, change the television channel or review the news on Facebook or Instagram, then they are discarded activities.

Rule #2: Your activity has to be individual

It is about improving your connection with your thoughts and managing to control them while maintaining your attention. However, when someone else catches your attention, the exercise is no longer effective.

Rule #3: Your activity can't be unhealthy

If the activity trains your attention but harms your health, the purpose of improving your life doesn't make sense. For example: eating unhealthy foods or smoking are activities that are discarded.

Now, if you accept the rules, you can continue reading to see the two main techniques to increase your concentration when creating your To-Do List.

Techniques to stay focused when creating your To-Do List

Technique #1: Choose a daily activity

Evaluate your daily routine and choose a simple activity (with a short duration) to which you can direct your attention fully for a few minutes (and that complies with the three rules you just read). That is, it is about being aware of what you are doing, directing all your attention and all your senses towards that activity for a short period of time.

These are some examples:

- ✓ Brush your teeth
- ✓ Wash the dishes
- ✓ Read a book
- ✓ Listen to music
- ✓ Make your bed
- ✓ Floss
- ✓ Draw or color
- ✓ Have a coffee or tea
- ✓ Read the newspaper
- ✓ Eat an apple

This type of activity can be done in a mindfulness way to help you to feel better, to enjoy the moment, and above all to train your mind to focus on only one thing at a time, controlling the impulse of distraction.

In this way, instead of training your mind to distract, you are doing the opposite: you are training your mind to concentrate. This long and short-term training helps you to have control of your thoughts when you really need to do it.

Technique #2: Identify your invading thoughts

Earlier on, I mentioned "types of distractions", where our thoughts are a type of internal distractions. You may wonder: what should I do during that activity to focus my attention? What do I do if thoughts or impulses suddenly arise?

If you detect any thought, concern, desire or impulse, simply identify that it is there, be aware of it and let it go. Gently return your attention to your activity.

For example, if you choose to wash your hair or brush your teeth and concentrate on that activity, but suddenly you start thinking about the numerous clothes that you need to wash for the day, then it means that your training is not working. You have to do be aware that thought appeared, then gently refocus on the movement of the brush or the cool water.

Little by little, you will learn to tame your mind. It's about not getting carried away by all the thoughts in your head, not trying to eliminate them.

Strategies

- ✓ When you have a task to complete, divide it into smaller and digestible tasks.

- ✓ Then take one of those sub-tasks, and write in a list form the sequence of steps you have to follow to complete it successfully.

- ✓ Mark as done according to the progress of each step.

- ✓ Don't write a list a mile long that you can never complete, or plan your day in such a way that you will be running from one place to another.

- ✓ Leave some space for breaks.

You are free to deviate from the course if necessary, but the structure of a general plan will help you keep your journey on the right track.

You will see how easy it is to avoid getting distracted because your mind gets hooked on the feeling of achievement and progress, which improves your productivity enormously.

In addition, this strategy gives you a feeling of "flow" or constant progress, which at the same time trains your ability to concentrate better and better.

Chapter 5: Tips to help save time in your daily tasks

Many times I have thought this myself. I don't have time for anything!

You have the feeling of always being in a hurry, not being able to cope, being very busy with many commitments, both professional and personal—but still you feel like you aren't moving forward, that you don't get to follow your goals or dreams. You don't do anything useful. You might also feel overwhelming, start many things and not finish them, or not know where to start… you wish the day had 40 hours! Has any of this ever happened to you?

If your answer is yes, don't despair, because in this chapter I am going to give you tips to save time in your daily tasks. Keep reading!

Three main tips to save time when doing daily tasks

Tip #1: Self-analysis. How do I spend my time?

Take a closer look at your day-to-day, the activities you do and the things that consume your time—take note of it. You can even use tools (which I recommend), such as TimeLogger or in a more labor-intensive Toggl context. This will help you build a strong foundation to reorganize yourself on.

Tip #2: Set a schedule for each task on your To-Do List

If there are tasks that require your attention every week, you can assign them to specific days and times. For example, issues such as accounting or reporting can be done within the same schedule every week. In this way, you will no longer have to look for a moment to do it, it will be enough to just meet the established schedule.

Tip #3: Check. Detect problems and look for solutions

There are some people who like the weekly plans and reviews, but the important thing is to do it every so often: check your agenda and evaluate how your week was. Have you done everything you wanted to? Are there items with bits missing? What happened?

You can detect problems and solve them in this way:

1. Did I fill my agenda with too many things for this day?
2. Did I define the objectives wrong?
3. Did I lack motivation? Did I make excuses not to do it?
4. Did I lack the energy or struggle to concentrate?
5. Did I prioritize other things that were not on the agenda or that distracted me?
6. Did it take me longer than expected?
7. Were there unforeseen circumstances?

This revision will make the next week's planning better, and you can work on the problems that prevented you from achieving your previous goals.

The difference between the urgent and the important

Do you know the story about the stones and the jar? What are your big stones? What are things important or priority? Family, health, friends, a hobby, intellectual concerns...?

<u>The Stones and the Failure</u>

One day, a motivator was giving a conference on time management to a group of professionals. To make a point clear, he used an example that professionals will never forget.

Standing in front of an audience of very successful people, he said, "I'd like to give you a little demonstration..."

From under the table, he took out a wide-mouthed glass jug and placed it on the table in front of him. Then, he took out a dozen fist-sized stones and began placing them one by one into the jug.

When the jug was full to the top and he couldn't place more stones, he asked the audience, "Is this jug full?"

All the attendees said, "Yes!"

Then he asked, "Are you sure?" Then he pulled out a bucket with smaller stones from under the table. He threw some of the stones into the jug and moved it, causing the small stones to settle into the empty space between the large ones.

When he had done this, he asked once more, "Is this jug full?"

This time, the audience was already guessing what was coming, so one of the attendees replied, "Probably not."

"Very well," the speaker answered. He pulled out a bucket full of sand from under the table and began throwing it into the jug. The sand settled into the space between the large stones and the small ones.

Once again, he asked the group, "Is this jug full?"

This time, several people answered in chorus, "No!"

Once again, the speaker said, "Very good!" Then he took out a jug full of water and poured water into the jug with stones, until it was full to the very edge. When he finished, he looked at the audience and asked, "What do you think the lesson of this little demonstration is?"

One of the spectators raised a hand and said, "It doesn't matter how full your schedule is—if you really try, you can always include more things."

"Of course not!" replied the speaker, "That's not it."

"The lesson is that if you don't put the big stones first, you can't put them in at any other time."

Often, we have many small urgent tasks at hand that leave us no place for the really important ones. We do a thousand things and still feel like we haven't done anything. Make a list of your "big stones", of the things that are important in your life. Then translate that into concrete actions that you can incorporate into your day-to-day life.

For example: call my Father every Tuesday at 8pm, go to yoga class on Saturdays at 10am, spend time with my son for half an hour when he gets home, have coffee with my friend Lucius, dedicate Sundays from 8pm to 9pm to writing poetry in my notebook ...

Conclusion

We have now reached the end of the journey of reading this book. What have you learned? Surely you have learned how to create a To-Do List that is effective following our step-by-step practical guide, strategies, tips, examples and techniques.

You have also learned how to manage your time when creating your To-Do-List. Now, reflect on this: What are the big stones in my life? Should I worry about my routine, what others think, the work I don't like? Or should I focus on my family, friends, moral values, health, the people I love and the things that make me happy? The biggest stones have to refer to your foundations, to the most important things for you, which are related to your values and affections, and which enriches as individuals.

In addition to our friends and family, time is the most valuable to us. We can earn more money, acquire wealth, but time is irreplaceable. As we get older, our finances become more secure, but time wanes; then time is the only thing that will matter to us. We can't replace the time, but we can save it and taste it.

If you really think about the importance of time, you will see the importance of having a To-Do List that really works. The truth is that no matter what medium you use to make your To-Do List, what really matters is the suitability and usefulness of it. The different aspects that must be done in the next few days or weeks must be arranged according to a common criterion.

Remember, if you follow our steps to create your To-Do List, you will avoid the stress that comes with having to remember everything you have to do. It will give you the satisfaction of fulfilling your activities and the assurance that you have not forgotten any task. It will allow you to organize your projects by setting defined objectives to help you effectively manage your time and improve your productivity.

*— **Magnus Muller***

About the author

Magnus Muller is a young writer who likes to explore the world as well as to play sports. He strongly believes that success can be attained with consistent hard work and effort.

He began writing his first book: **"The 5 Minute Procrastination Addiction Cure"**, to help those who suffer from procrastination to overcome it by just using a simple rule of thumb. He has now also published his second and third book: **"The 5 Minute To-Do List Formula"** and **"The 5 Minute Mindfulness Practical Guide"** to help his readers achieve their goals.

These 3 books come together to form **"The 5 Minute Self Help Series"**. Since these 3 books are of different topics, hence you do not need to read them in chronological order but start with any book of your choice.

To find out more about his work, check out his books at **https://amazon.com/author/magnusmuller** and you will start to enjoy more free time and accomplish your tasks!

Leave a review

If you truly enjoy this book, please help to leave a review on Amazon! This book is now available in both the kindle and paperback version.

Kindle: https://www.amazon.com/dp/B07F8HFDLC
Paperback: https://www.amazon.com/dp/1983360260
Author: https://amazon.com/author/magnusmuller

The 5 Minute Self Help Series

The 5 Minute Self Help Series (Book 1)

The 5 Minute Procrastination Addiction Cure
Eliminating Procrastination By Starting In 5 Minutes Or Less

By Magnus Muller

Kindle: http://www.amazon.com/dp/B07CT215ZZ
Paperback: http://www.amazon.com/dp/1983161640

The 5 Minute Self Help Series (Book 2)

The 5 Minute To-Do List Formula
A Diagrammatic Guide To Complete Your Task Within 2 Weeks

By Magnus Muller

Kindle: http://www.amazon.com/dp/B07F8HFDLC
Paperback: http://www.amazon.com/dp/1983360260

The 5 Minute Self Help Series (Book 3)

The 5 Minute Mindfulness Practical Guide
20 Simple Habits To Lead A Stress Free Life, Reduce Anxiety And Treat Depression

By Magnus Muller

Kindle: http://www.amazon.com/dp/B07F8H6ZS2
Paperback: http://www.amazon.com/dp/1983360392

Check out other books

5 Steps Self Discipline Blueprint
Resist Temptations, Get Things Done and Lead the
Live You Desire

By Trevor Henry

Kindle: https://www.amazon.com/dp/B07FLWHM3D
Paperback: https://www.amazon.com/dp/171778903X

Printed in Great Britain
by Amazon